BROKEN LINES

BROKEN LINES

POEMS

Sugar le Fae

REBEL SATORI PRESS
NEW ORLEANS & NEW YORK

Published in the United States of America by
Rebel Satori Press
www.rebelsatoripress.com

Cover Art: Amy Wright, "Pearl and the Swallow-tailed Comet"

Paperback ISBN: 978-1-60864-334-9

Contents

Greenwood Avenue

In those days, my poems were filled with blue jeans and sex dreams, stars so sharp, they hurt the sky. I lived in Clarksville, TN, near the university, on the safer end of Greenwood, before the minimart gave way to meth dens toward the Confederate cemetery.

My best friend lived across the street. Any day of the week, but especially Sunday afternoons, we drank 40s and smoked blunts on his front porch. I lived above a creepy, old landlord who nightly sat naked on his dark porch-swing watching us party.

My penchant for straight men was legendary. The tussled, chain-smoking poet. The keen, philosopher twink. The narcissistic, army vet. Each one married a woman. The details blur together. My apologies. In those days, I was still chasing after my father.

1.
NIGHTSTANDS

Jesse James

I dreamed you a cowboy once
in a lacquered saddle. You straddled
a high horse, your face unshaven,
your hands a man's, your hips
a hinge on haunches.
                    For days,
we waited without rain. The tracks,
a bassline buried in arid earth.
The train, a star soprano late to stage.
We slept on horsecloth. Cassiopeia inked
her M in the west. *Maybe it means
moonshine or money?* was all
                    you thought to say.

Morning four, we boarded the beast,
bandanas bound behind our ears.
                    The old conductor
crouched in a corner, the coal shovel
cocked off his ribs like a rifle
breaking both his thumbs in the scuffle.

We fucked on bags of bank bills
to smell wealthy. You asked again
about Cassiopeia. *Maybe her M's a W?
Maybe she just points west.*
                    But I didn't know,
so I shot you twice between the eyes.

Cool

The way the cattle-fence
held the fog at bay
that rose over the pastures
those nights we reclined
on lawn-chairs behind
your house, sharing beer
instead of kissing.

Cool, your messy hair
and brooding scowl, your
peacoat and Marlboros,
your poems about bellowing
old men on bicycles,
your father who died while
you were in high school.

Cool, your cat's blue
shadow crossing the fence
against fog and starlight,
your hand close enough to
touch, and in the fields,
invisible, the lesbian cattle
cuddling for warmth.

Achilles in Clarksville

I wouldn't survive the world you endured,
the doors you torched, the children
you saved from slave-traders—
Violence, I abhor. But sometimes,
I envy the bonds between men at war.
That raw communion in the desert
far from civilian inhibitions.

Men for whom the stars are always sharp.
Had I served beside you, instead of
writing you poems from home,
we would've been Bonnie and Clyde.
One of us, at least, would've died
for the other. We would've been lovers;
our letters would've been bestsellers.

But you came back to a wife and daughter.
To Clarksville, where you used to
badmouth soldiers when I knew you.
I miss your loudness in crowds of men,
your homemade, rope flip-flops.
You came back minus your baby-fat,
but whatever you lost, it wasn't weight.

Narcissus Revisited

When you said you needed me
to help you understand love,
but really, you wanted me
to save your marriage, I had to
show you why you came.
We love a man, on the verge
of divorcing his wife, crawling
into bed with an old friend.
You thought I'd be on her side.
So did I, but my loyalties lie
with you, like we're lying now
in a knot in our underwear.
I meant it, when I told you not
to die before we had an affair.

Clownfish

—after Britney Spears

My feelings for you are like the incestuous
loneliness of the sea anemone. To be all-feeling
is its own hell. The dull charge of my desire
killing me, a tangy numbness humming
me to musical filaments, tingling till
I sting in all directions. Everyone but you
must beware of my bioelectric mermaid hair.
Confess, it's thrilling to brush against my buzz!
I shiver sometimes, thinking about how
still you can be so close to me: so bright it hurts.
Believe it or not, you're the only one.

Astronaut Blues

In a thousand thousand years,
when the sun's licked
Mercury to a Hershey's kiss,
and Venus blinks
oblivion, you'll still be
married to someone else.
When Earth's oceans boil off,
and we flee in starships
sailing on solar wind
to Jupiter's moons—
she'll cling to you through
the asteroid belt's
sandpit of broken glass.
Even when we land,
foreign on a frozen ocean,
begin again, and
maybe humanity can
survive a few more chapters,
even then, I'm thinking:
This at last will make him love me.

Him

The temp at the front desk
snaps me back into my body.
His warm bass repeating
greetings. His Ninja Turtle t-.
I settle an empty table
and open a book of poems
so lush it seems a fever-dream.
We look each other over
like books. Our week-
old beards. My rainbow beads.
His mittens' pink stripes
as he readies to leave.
This is what I want to keep.
Those last glances back.
The brief relief from anguish.
Having come upon the fire
of a stranger in the dark,
dead-tired and with a secret.

Brando on Pryor

He'd taken to calling me Brandy
at this or that premier or club.
Most folks don't know, but Richard
loved to dance. He'd get lit
and tear up the floor. It was joyful
to watch. His salamander body
popping and stepping. His green

leisure suit. That irrepressible smile
no beat could crack. After a few
drinks, I'd join him. Richard danced
at you, not with you, cigarette in hand.
And that smile, bright as a bowl
of oranges, that was his edge.
We were notorious in some clubs

for our dance-offs. All the brandies
I choked down for the sake of a joke!
In close quarters, we were gentler
than either one expected, softer.
Don't poke his afro though.
Rich was a stranger by the time he lit
himself on fire, but I believe it.

Lucifer

Beauty made you proud, so I threw you to the ground.
—Ezekiel 28:17

I first met Lucifer the day he left
his second wife, a self-made architect

who took him to Kenya, where he slept
with a machete under his bed.

Then to Scotland, where he was one
more shitty American. They had a son.

They liked to drink. Both his wives
vociferously disliked Satan's bisexuality.

He's part-Cherokee if he can believe
his gun-nut father, who got drunk

and beat him up, whom he still loves.
Goes by Luke now because

Luke means light. His fingers glisten
like opera gloves. Stars sharpen

their gills. Shirtless in a wicker chair,
he asks me where he should sleep.

Red horns poke through his trucker hat.
When I offer my bed, he agrees.

Tennessee Pink

In walks John Wilkes Booth,
sporting a tailored blazer
and trim trousers, handsome
as the day he shot Lincoln.
Over one eye, an eye-
patch fashion accessory.
       Pivoting patrons,
he sidles up to the bar,
orders a whiskey and water.
Friday night. Kajuns
is packed. *Boys in the Band*
had let out down the street.
       Flick of the wrist,
his mustache meets his fist
at a bone-white cigarette.
He was meant to be a writer,
he tells the bartender,
sipping his drink…
       Goes by the name
of Tennessee Pink.
He's here for the same
reason as all the rest—
It's karaoke night,
and he's next. Tonight,
he sings "I Shot the Sheriff."

Handing Him His Poem

He didn't like it like I liked it
so he left,
late for work as it is.
His car's harsh start splintered
the winter air.
I leapt from where
I hadn't slept, barefoot
to the front porch, shirtless
by the steps,
then, in only underwear,
jerked his door ajar
to his hands, his arms.
Here. I wrote this for you.

You Didn't Just Come Here to Die

Those last few days, he stole
away for a moment alone
with each of us. Me, he asked
to meet in the olive grove.
I was sniffling like a boy
and couldn't look him in the eye.
He took my hand and led me
on. The garden opened
like a wound. We've been friends
since one of us could play girl,
he said, laughing. Judas—
But I was already kissing him,
tearing at his tunic to feel
the heat and heave of his chest.
Pressed up against me,
breathless beneath silver trees,
he chanted low I love yous
until they dragged him away.

2.
ARS POETICA

"Nor is it clear why he writes poetry—
whether he pissed on his father's ashes
or defiled a sacred lightning strike…"
—Horace, *The Art of Poetry*

Madame Sosostris Hits
Menopause Childless

Madame Sosostris bares for me
the new boobs she bought half-off
from LSU's student surgeon program.
          And she's right—
her right breast is visibly larger.
"Either way," I say, "they look good!"
          "Thanks hun," she says,
shouldering her silk kimono.
Blue smoke swims from her ashtray.
She switched at 50 to herbal cigarettes
          like actors smoke in movies.
"Today's my granddad's birthday,"
she says, gesturing to the bookshelf.
"He made that ceramic head."
"A self-portrait, no doubt," I say,
          lifting the sinister face of an elf.
"He always said we were descended
from a race of super-beings," she says.
"He shot himself before he hit 50.
          When I was a kid…
he taught me how to not blink."

Emily Dickinson's Missing Kitten

It's funny, the things you can keep—
      Hidden. History won't remember
      The kitten I tended on the edge
Of the field, for instance, half-dead
By the daffodils' upturned yellow death-
Bells. How I nursed her back to health—
      Brought water in a bowl, a thimble
      Of milk, fish-skins to lick—
How she bounded back! Her tiger-stripes!—
      Her gray fur flashing white!—
      How she leapt into the unshorn
Grass toward whatever barn-loft
Or church rafter her parents prowl—
Still strangers after all
         these litters.

Blank Verse With Blue Notes

If ever I find you crying in your own dark car,
knowing you solely through grad-school's
keyhole, and I knock on the passenger door

and ask if you're okay, and pausing, you shake
your head, and I ask why, and you say you
don't know if you're getting a divorce, and we

decide to drive to the only café in town
that's not a Waffle House and order us a coke
and a chocolate milk, and the waitress asks

if you're okay, and we nod and smile in sync;
if after she turns, I ask you why, and you say he
wants you to quit school and move north,

I won't hesitate to say, He doesn't deserve you.
Poem, take note. Speak the clichés you mean.

Letter to a Lost Pen

I'm waiting in the graveyard
with mud the color of red-velvet cake.
I would not tattoo you on my arm,
but I'll hold you when you want me to.

Since you left, my markers run dry
or bleed my books to bruises.
But you, all you do is rest or write.
I could love a man like that.

Now's the hour for first flowers,
the sad parade of last year's pinecones.
Don't wait too late to find me,
pen-pal! You'll miss the daffodils.

Keats' Grave

Poets return to Rome
as cats to stalk their own
headstones. Keats
sleeps easy under cover
of an umbrella pine,
lets me scratch his ears.

I've come to see,
in the Non-Catholic
Cemetery, *Here lies one*
whose name was writ in water
etched on his grave
in the shade of a pyramid.
It shakes me to think
that my tears are the ink.

Percy Shelley's heart
(the part that didn't burn)
beats out for Keats
a field apart. (Mary kept
the rest in her desk,
wrapped in his poesy.)

He drowned with Keats'
book in his pocket
—who'd traded locks
with that Adonis.
Wild jasmine ravages
the walls of their graveyard.
The pyramid sleeps
between them like a cat.

Burning Percy's Body

Because of quarantine, they had to burn
the body where it washed up on the beach
unrecognizable in Tuscany,
stripped of flesh from the face and hands
after a week in the sink.
                    Townsfolk
noted the book in his pocket, though none
touched him for fear. Masked men with sticks
managed, after a few tries, to flip him
on his back, away from the tide
—kinder than the sea had left him.

They built an upturned boat above him
taller, until the tinder cathedral
peaked to a pyramid with him at the heart.
Each man lit a match, his favorite part.

Dream of the Muse

I'm Rilke
in the arms of Orpheus,
stunned into silence
in an alpine glen.
Pulse thrumming my ears,
my own dumb panting.
He covers my nakedness

in a white jacket.
He can hardly bear
to look at me.
Birds, squirrels, even
flowers lean in to listen.
He lifts me like a wife.
(His static cling!)

My pale legs dangling
from his arms' dark wings.
Squirrels take flight,
but birds stay to watch.
Gripping his neck, I can feel
where once
it was severed.

—after Thomas Terceira's "Metamorphosis 2"

Ganymede's Rise
—*after Ovid*

Jupiter, the king above, burned
with love for the Trojan stud,
and so found a form he preferred
to his own, though no bird
but one was worth turning into.
None but an eagle could bear
his thunderbolts (and a Trojan too).

Without delay, beating the air
with phantasmagorical feathers,
he snatched him away—the twink
who even now mixes drinks
and administers nectar to Jove
against the will of his sister-wife.

Since You Believe Everything You Read,

—after Catullus

I'll pound your ass, Aurelius, you slut,
and Furius, you cunt, I'll fuck your mouth.
You think you know me cuz you've read my stuff?
Conflate the poet and the speaker much?
      We agree that poets should be decent
people, but their verses needn't be.
In fact, most poems are worth their salt
      because they're sexy or lack decency.
Poems that itch like stitched incisions.
I speak not to twinks—who cares!—but to bears
      who can't handle their own erections!
You, who've read thousands of my kisses, dare
to claim I'm not a man / that *I'm* the fag?
I'll fuck you till you squeal, then I'll make you gag.

Cleopatra Considering
Her Cat, the Moon

Her eyes are marbles I forgot
I lost. Her ears are flickering moths.
The heights she climbs to notice ghosts
I don't!—Let her lick the butter!

You picked her, Jules, said
she reminded you of me: so young
to be so gray—and now you've left me
to name her. Her sister, you brought
home to Rome, call her Venus.

My Luna is living alabaster—
white where her belly meets her teats.
The woman who sold her told you
Bastet painted a fishbone down her back
to encourage her to worship Hygiene.

Darling, she licks her nipples pink
in your absence! Even sleeping,
she kneads my womb to a hymnal rhythm.
I named her Luna after *your* moon, Julio,
you've yet to introduce me to…

"A Perfectly Erotic Half-Hour"

I never had you, nor will I ever have you,
Cavafy wrote of you for me
a century before we were born.
You kept my half-smoked packs of cloves
in your junk-drawer, but what for?
Whatever we were, we were more than
stoner poets debating favorite Blake engravings.

Fast-forward to the 4th of July,
to swordfights in the yard with the guys,
their whiskey breath and stained-glass tattoos.
To sparklers duct-taped to arrows
protracted at the dark stars like flares.

To the cardboard mortar, the egg-crates
of shells, the smells of gunpowder and burnt hair.
But we who serve Art with intensity of mind
create pleasure / which almost seems real,
this hundred-year-old poem proposes.
It knows us, the red shell I hand you like an apple.

Love, an Abstract

His torso's door gnashing ravenously,
the Tin Man chases
chest-first after the heart floating
an arm's length out of reach
            in his own hand.

3.
END TIMES: ALMANAC

Last Light

Now is the twilight.
Now is the brightest
of the end-times.
Brighter by degrees
than moonlight.
When shades of trees
mean darkness.

Dusk is just blush,
wine-flush, a bruise.
Haze to hide us
from the stars.
Dull, purple mist
lifts in the cool.
We're on the cusp

of nightfall,
in the afterglow.
When you have to
start riding home.
Gnats take a last pass.
The moon's blacks
are still blue.

Like Penelope

I nightly undo
this fuse
of maleness
I've been tied to.
Every day,
weaving
and grieving
my own noose.
This rope
soaked
in moonshine.
This leash
grown into me.
All night,
I pluck petals.
Is this knot
what they mean
by loyalty?

Patience

Once, when we were mice,
still scared of the sun, we lived
among dinosaurs.

Every night, we drank
the cold rain from their footprints,
browsing nuts and bugs.

We slept through thunder,
fire, hailstorms, woke on worlds
of fallen flowers.

Moonlight ripened us,
rounded us to wheels of cheese.
Darkness warmed our blood.

Back when we were mice,
we slept in dens with our friends,
licked each other clean.

Because our bodies
made heat, milk, fat, fur, we lived.
We could wait our turn.

Death Ballad

Death shone bright today
  like a girl whose fever broke.
  Like a friendly stray,
  Death met me on the road.

Death walked me to town
  to buy beer and butter.
  Death sat on the ground
  with the cats at the butcher.

Death whistled at a man
  in the street who didn't hear.
  Death patted my back
  when I choked on my beer.

Death followed me home
  like a lover's perfume.
  And though I said 'No,'
  Death came into my room.

Medusa

At best, there are flecks
of yourself
that you can't bear
to look at,
white hot suns
that can't be unseen.
At best,
you have to swing out
your whole life
from behind your shield's
silver mirror
at the snakes in your own hair.
The rest of your story
is spent
wearing them out
in the open,
the clothes you sewed
from your skin.

Abraham

We followed the river to mountains.
For years, we walked upstream.
With a reed, I wrote stars into clay.
With my hands, I measured the hours.

Milk. Knife. River. Earth.
I wrote them over and over.
For a hundred years, we were barren.
My wife little more than a sliver.

The Bull of Heaven foretells flood.
Ice-melt swells with the moon.
My body is the mud I cut from the river.
The stars I write are scars.
Every night, I slaughter a lamb
to save my son from my own hand.

The Bit in Bitter

This taut knot turned
pearl in the pit and
pendulum of my hips
—the grit inside it
is a grain of obsidian,
a single spider egg.
It wears me like a chain.
A bead, a bitter seed.
It dangles like genitals.
Someday, when they
pull me from the oven,
they'll find it, hard
and black as buckshot.
And kicking it under
the furnace on accident,
the cremator's son
will check for it once,
twice, then shrug it off.

Lady of Ephesus

Lady of Ephesus,
immaculate daughter
—best to the least of us!
Bless this altar!

Virgin-mother, goddess
of paradox, wetnurse
to the thirsty—
Lend us your purse!

Huntress of injustice,
suckle us better!
Many-breasted midwife,
loose your dark stars!

The Infant Jesus Speaks

The throes of labor drove her to the trunk of a palm.
Oh, she cried, that I had died, and been a thing forgot!
—Quran 19:23

Mary to the desert drove
alone to die of shame,
but when she wept,
a date-palm crept
and covered her in shade.

Mary in a dairy slept,
a cave where men kept game.
Where Mary tread,
her unborn led.
When Mary bled, it rained.

Mary then to Bethlehem
returned to clear her name.
They stoned her dead
except Christ said,
Let he who's without blame!

Orion

Zeus nailed him to the sky
blind, crucified, flayed,
hung by his belt in the rain,
stung by a giant scorpion,
and still, he hunts his sisters.

Egypt named him Osiris,
whose blood was the flood,
whose wife was a bright bird
rising from the river reeds
to piece back his body.

That's the way with seasons.
Birth, murder, rape, death.
I never knew the myths.
When I looked, I saw
Michael Jackson dancing.

New Moon

Broken bones of heroes
crowd the sun down,
mixed in with their foes
and lovers, parents
and pets, as if the afterlife
were just / some field
where a city once thrived,
last world's last remains,
invisible in daylight,
distant and mysterious
enough to be meaningful
to disparate nations,
whose cities, from above,
resemble constellations.

Eclipse

The moon moves away from us
as slowly as fingernails grow.
Once, it orbited so close,
the ocean could almost lick it.
So close, it could hide
a quarter of the sky, whole
seasons of constellations.
So, when you grow up and decide
the world isn't magic after all,
remember the incredible
shrinking moon, impossibly old,
that fits like a thumb over the sun
just for you, human.

B-SIDES

Pan

I didn't notice till the night
you left: your horns and cloven hooves,
your chest's relative hairlessness.

Embarrassing, not knowing
a satyr when you meet one, the sad clod
who couldn't tell an angel…

Bandits had beaten you bad,
bruised your bare skin black.
I offered to shave off your mane.

But one does want something
to tug on, you said, twirling
the curl at your nape like a girl.

You were right to suspect me
trying to make you a man. / Forgive me.

Straight Waiting

All the straight waiters at work
make it a point to touch me
once a shift at least, to treat me
to the same fraternal gestures:
the shoulder-hold, the fist-bump,
one of those inane handshakes
they dole out in high school
        I still can't seem to do.
Robert, the elder waiter, prefers
a gentle backslap. Dominic,
of "pure French Creole" stock,
backhands my bicep all shift,
        chirpin' "Ya heard me?"
Marquis, one of the bussers,
bulldozes my shoulder blades
        with his forehead.
When I point out this straight
male propensity for physical
affection to Dinos, he says
        "You're just saying that
cuz you're gay," and he's right;
that doesn't make me wrong.

Wanted Ad

Don't write for me a sonnet that couldn't
accommodate the cadences of names—
Emily Dickinson's delicate
dactyls or Edna St. Vincent Millay's sway.
Any clever poet can write iamb
after iamb, aping the god of Moses
or René Descartes. Don't write *me* a poem
with artless rhyme or that's shapeless.
Write me a sonnet that's a composition
of competence. Mind the page like a frame,
breaking lines with intention.
Marry meaning with music. In my name,
write neither porn nor scripture—
but like a calligrapher signing their signature.

Dream (2)

I'm Sam from *Bewitched*.
Except I'm in prison
without powers.
Like me, my cell is small
and white. Beyond
the bars, angry inmates
bark and catcall.
I close a sliding door
against the noise.
My blonde coif intact,
I wiggle my nose,
but nothing happens.
Endora arrives in a sea-
foam sequin gown
also without powers
and escorts me to a cab.
At home, nothing
feels right. I'm living
on set, without ceilings.
I can hear Darrin
in the den, watching
sports with a coworker.
Turns out, it's both
Darrins, drunk on beer,
one with a mind
to seduce the other.
What's going on here?

The Tanner's Wife

For more generations than memory,
we farmed these fields at the edge
of the steppes, tamed the grain
and the cattle that ate it.
At four, I watched my father strip
the skin from a young bull
hung up by its quarters,
the muscle glistening above snow.
Stretched and shorn, the hide
sat in urine till it turned
soft as the curd we traded
from mountain herders.
That's the memory I'm left with
a hundred generations later.
When they dug me up in China,
my hair was still red
and sinuous as naked muscle.
But my skin, in tribute, had tanned.

Judith Among the Men

Listen, I'm about to do something no one will forget.
—Judith 8:32

When Judith heard her kinsmen
doubt that God could deliver them,
she snuck into their captor's den,
          befriended, then beheaded him.
Returning to her kin, she said,
Behold! God is good! and held up
the warlord's hideous grin.
          It might've been Medusa's head
for the stony stares she met.
Scripture claims they celebrated
Judith, but someone paid her debt.
          A widow, she never remarried;
the men wouldn't let her forget.
They too deserved her knife-edge.

Loonie

Backing under the shower's hot spittle,
a metal knuckle knocks and settles
on the bathtub floor. A loonie?
Must've swam up my pajama pants
and stuck to my butt. What booty
to excavate from one's own bathtub,
stamped with a bust of the queen mum!

What strange delight to meet her
here in the shower, to turn her over,
warm from the steam (and the heat of my bum).
To find on her back, a duck floating
under scratched brass mountains
and a maple leaf moon—a mallard,
perhaps—no, obviously a loon.

How nice to set her on the windowsill
gently, intently, heads-up. To lift her
again at the end, cold from the sill's still
water, her icy stare steady if sweaty,
the metal of house keys, bullets, bells.
Yes, to love her for her character—
not just for what she could get me.
The Coke she buys tastes like a miracle.

Casualty

I've started thinking of
my shower concerts
as performances
before God, naked,
unafraid in front
of my maker,
recorded live for
review in the afterlife
waiting room.

Notes

All translations are mine except where noted.

"Blank Verse with Blue Notes" is for Ashley Joy.

"Madame Sosostris Hits Menopause Childless" is a nod to T.S. Eliot's "famous clairvoyante... / With a wicked pack of cards" from *The Waste Land*.

"A Perfectly Erotic Half-Hour" quotes the C.P. Cavafy poem "Half Hour," tr. Keeley and Sherrard.

"Ganymede's Rise" is more-or-less faithful to the Latin from Ovid's *Metamorphoses*, Book 10.

"Since You Believe Everything You Read" is a playful translation of Catullus' infamous "Carmen 16."

"Death Ballad," commissioned by Kat Dehring, lifts its first line from the ancient Egyptian text *A Debate Between a Man and His Soul*, tr. Wilson.

"Loonie" is for Keith Maillard.

SPECIAL THANKS to Amy Wright for her guidance and generosity over the years.

To my Clarksville crew, now dispersed, whose love and community made many of these poems possible, especially Sienna Finney, Alexis Alexander, Myron Blaine, Nick Wood, Erica Vaught, Sally Sarah, Brandt and Aurora Hardin, and many others.

To the unnamed ex-lovers, and to my younger self for having the time and energy for love poetry.

To all my mothers, sisters, and aunties. Thank you.

In memory of all my grandmothers.

Acknowledgments

My sincerest thanks to the journals and magazines that first published some of these poems:

30 Poets, 30 Poems	"Achilles in Clarksville"
Arc Magazine	"You Didn't Just Come Here"
The Albion Review	"Jesse James"
Assaracus	"The Bit in Bitter"
	"Emily Dickinson's Missing"
	"Since You Believe"
	"Wanted Ad"
Eleven Eleven	"Ganymede's Rise"
Event Magazine	"Tennessee Pink"
	"Blank Verse"
The Gay & Lesbian Review	"Brando on Pryor"
Lemon Hound	"Clownfish"
	"Love, an Abstract"
The Maynard	"Straight Waiting"
Plenitude	"Madame Sosostris"
	"Pan"
	"Loonie"
The Puritan	"Astronaut Blues"
RFD	"Keat's Grave"
untethered	"Cleopatra Considering"

Activist, educator, musician, and prize-winning poet, Sugar le Fae (PhD) has taught English and writing for two decades; served as a Poetry Editor of *Five Points*, *PRISM international*, and other literary journals; and published widely; most recently, a verse memoir, *The Mustard Seed* (April Gloaming Press 2023). Follow Sugar on Instagram @sugar_lefae.